A gift of the
Peruvian Park PTA

Flamingos

By Jodie Shepherd

Children's Press®

An Imprint of Scholastic Inc.

Nature's CHILDREN™

Content Consultant
Becky Ellsworth
Curator, Shores
Columbus Zoo and Aquarium

Library of Congress Cataloging-in-Publication Data
Names: Shepherd, Jodie, author.
Title: Flamingos / by Jodie Shepherd.
Description: New York : Children's Press, an imprint of Scholastic Inc.,
   2019. | Series: Nature's children | Includes bibliographical references
   and index.
Identifiers: LCCN 2018027200| ISBN 9780531127759 (library binding) | ISBN
   9780531128992 (paperback)
Subjects: LCSH: Flamingos--Juvenile literature.
Classification: LCC QL696.C56 S54 2019 | DDC 598.3/5

Design by Anna Tunick Tabachnik

Creative Direction: Judith E. Christ for Scholastic Inc.

Produced by Spooky Cheetah Press

Printed in Heshan, China   62

SCHOLASTIC, CHILDREN'S PRESS, NATURE'S CHILDREN™, and associated logos
are trademarks and/or registered trademarks of Scholastic Inc.

1 2 3 4 5 6 7 8 9 10 R 28 27 26 25 24 23 22 21 20 19

Scholastic Inc., 557 Broadway, New York, NY 10012.

Photographs ©: cover: Hitesh Parmar/EyeEm/Getty Images; 1: retales botijero/Getty Images; 4 leaf silo and throughout:
stockgraphicdesigns.com; 4 top: Jim McMahon/Mapman®; 5 child silo: All-Silhouettes.com; 5 flamingo silo: Alekseeva Yulia/
Shutterstock; 5 bottom: estivillml/iStockphoto; 6 flamingo silo and throughout: Miceking/Shutterstock; 7: PHOTO BY PRASIT
CHANSAREEKORN/Getty Images; 8: Laurent Renaud/Biosphoto; 11: cyoginan/iStockphoto; 12: Connie Stahl/EyeEm/Getty
Images; 15: Ben Hall/NPL/Minden Pictures; 16 top left: Martin Harvey/Getty Images; 16 top right: Piotr Naskrecki/Minden
Pictures; 16 bottom left: MZPHOTO.CZ/Shutterstock; 16 bottom right: Ingo Jezierski/Alamy Images; 19: blickwinkel/Alamy
Images; 20: Juan Carlos Munoz/Nature Picture Library/Getty Images; 23: ivanmateev/iStockphoto; 25: Franck Fouquet/
Biosphoto/Minden Pictures; 26: Gerry Ellis/Minden Pictures; 29: ZSSD/Minden Pictures; 30: Murat Öner Ta/Anadolu Agency/
Getty Images; 33: Ghedoghedo/Wikimedia; 34: Lorraine Boogich/iStockphoto; 37: De Agostini/G. Nimatallah/The Granger
Collection; 38: FabVietnam_Photography/iStockphoto; 41: Sergio Pitamitz/Robert Harding Picture Library; 42 bottom:
AndreAnita/Shutterstock; 42 center left: Angiolino Baruffa/Shutterstock; 42 top: Stefan Holm/Dreamstime; 42 center right:
Joel Sartore, National Geographic Photo Ark/Getty Images; 43 left: cyoginan/iStockphoto; 43 bottom right: Eric Isselee/Getty
Images; 43 top right: Lorraine Boogich/iStockphoto.

◀ Cover image
shows greater
flamingos wading
in a lake in India.

Table of Contents

Fact File: Flamingos

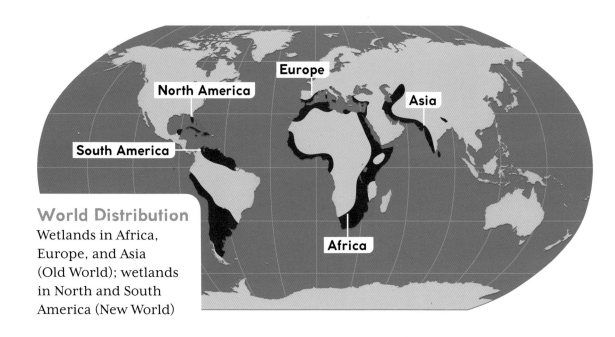

Europe

North America

Asia

South America

Africa

World Distribution
Wetlands in Africa, Europe, and Asia (Old World); wetlands in North and South America (New World)

Habitat
Coastal wetlands, lakes, muddy lagoons, the mouths of rivers

Habits
Live in large colonies; like to wade in shallow, salty water; often stand on one leg

Diet
Algae, plankton, and other small seafood

Distinctive Features
Long neck and legs; mostly pink feathers with some black; curved beaks

Fast Fact
Male flamingos are almost always bigger than females.

Average Size

**4 ft. 6 in.
(1.4 m)**

Human (age 10)

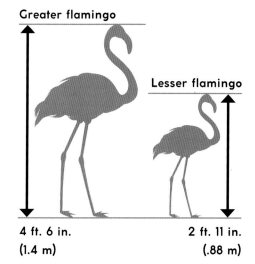

Greater flamingo

Lesser flamingo

**4 ft. 6 in.
(1.4 m)**

**2 ft. 11 in.
(.88 m)**

Flamingos (adults)

Classification

CLASS
Aves
(birds)

ORDER
Phoenicopteriformes
(flamingos)

FAMILY
Phoenicopteridae
(flamingos)

GENUS & SPECIES
Old World
- *Phoenicopterus roseus*
  (greater flamingo)
- *Phoeniconaias minor*
  (lesser flamingo)

New World
- *Phoenicopterus chilensis*
  (Chilean flamingo)
- *Phoenicoparrus andinus*
  (Andean flamingo)
- *Phoenicoparrus jamesi*
  (James's or puna
  flamingo)
- *Phoenicopterus ruber*
  (American or
  Caribbean flamingo)

◀ **Andean flamingo**

5

CHAPTER 1

Fantastic Flamingos

Whoosh! A huge pink cloud takes off from the shallow lake and rises into the sky. Honks, squawks, grunts, and growls fill the air. It's a flock of flamingos looking for a new feeding spot. With their long necks stretched out in front of them, their long legs stretched out behind, and their wide wings stretched out to each side, they're a fantastic sight to see.

The word *flamingo* comes from the Latin word *flamma*, which means flame. When you see the thousands of pink feathers in a flock of flamingos, it's easy to see how these birds got their name. A flock can also be called a colony, or a flamboyance, a word that means colorful showiness. It fits perfectly, as flamingos are famous for their showy pink color!

▶ Flamingos are almost always found in a crowd.

Fast Fact
Andean and James's flamingos have three toes; other species have four.

Around the World

There are six different kinds, or **species**, of flamingos. The greater and lesser flamingos belong to what's called the Old World flamingo family. They live in Africa, Europe, and Asia. The greater flamingo is the largest of all flamingos, and the lesser flamingo is the smallest. The other four species are called New World flamingos. They live in North and South America.

There are small differences in size and appearance among the species. Some of their behaviors and habits may be a little different, too, depending on where they live. But no matter which species, when you see one flamingo, you are sure to see many others! Whether wading, swimming, or flying, flamingos stick together in large groups called colonies. They are very social animals.

◄ Almost two million flamingos flock together in Tanzania, East Africa.

Some Body!

Flamingos are easy to recognize. They have many features that make them stand out from other birds.

A flamingo's long, thin neck is made up of 19 different bones. Human necks have only seven! All of those bones make it easy for the birds to bend and twist their necks—something they do a lot. Flamingos often sleep with their heads resting on their backs, tucked beneath some feathers for warmth.

Like all wading birds, flamingos have long legs. Most species have pink or orange legs, but the legs of Andean flamingos are bright yellow. You probably think that the joint about halfway up the leg is a knee. It's actually an ankle. So half of what we think of as the bird's leg is really its foot! The flamingos' knees are hidden under the feathers at the top of their legs.

Flamingo beaks are large and curved. They are made from keratin. That's the same material human fingernails are made from.

Fast Fact
A flamingo's brain is smaller than its eyeball!

Neck
is made up of 19 bones that make it easy to bend and twist in all directions.

Pink Feathers
are what flamingos are famous for. They're beautiful— and waterproof, too!

Curved Beak
is deep and large to scoop up food and water.

Long Thin Legs
may be yellow, orange, or pink, depending on the species.

Webbed Feet
make it easy to paddle in the water, as well as walk on sand and soft mud.

11

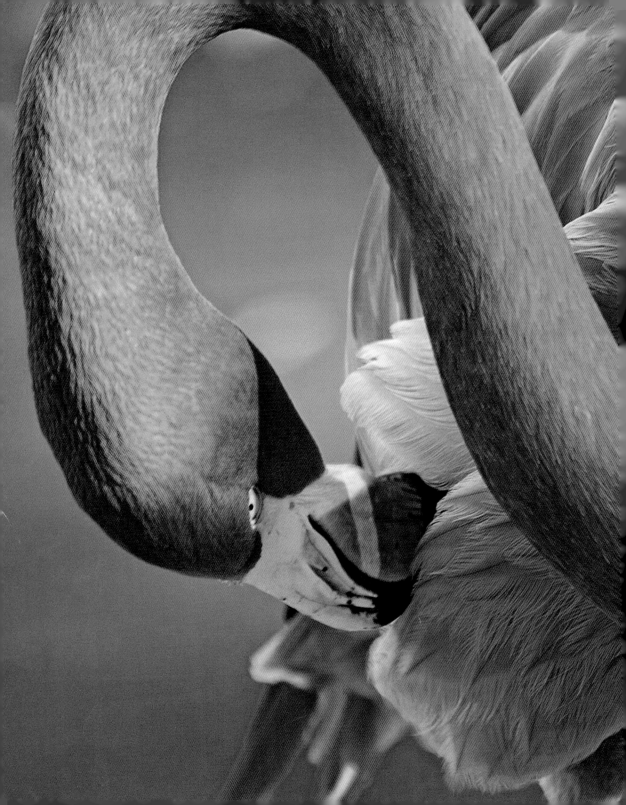

Pretty in Pink

Flamingos are famous for their pink color. Each species is a different shade. The greater flamingos are the palest, and the American flamingos are the brightest. Flamingos may spend up to one-third of their day **preening**, or grooming, their beautiful feathers.

A flamingo's pink color comes from the shellfish and algae it eats. These foods are rich in substances called carotenoids. Carotenoids are also found in carrots, beets, and other foods that humans eat—though we don't eat enough of them to turn us pink! But flamingos aren't *only* pink. They have black flight feathers, too, which you see only when the birds fly. And they have yellow eyes. Of course, the birds' bright colors make **camouflage** hard. It's easy for **predators** to find them.

Flamingo feathers aren't just pretty. They are also waterproof. A **gland** near the bird's tail produces oil, which covers the feathers and keeps the flamingo warm in the water.

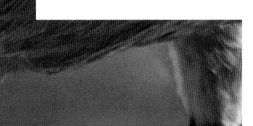

◀ Birds with well-groomed, bright feathers are more attractive to mates.

CHAPTER 2

Living Wild

Flamingos spend their lives in warm **wetlands**, including muddy **lagoons**, coastal wetlands, and **estuaries**, the places where rivers empty into the sea. They especially like soda lakes. Don't be fooled by the name! A soda lake is filled with salt, not soda. Flamingos like to gather on the salt islands that form in the middle of soda lakes.

The Chilean, James's, and Andean flamingos make their homes high up in South America's soaring Andes Mountains. In the cooler mountain temperatures, they may flock together near hot springs to keep warm.

Flamingos don't **migrate** like many other birds do. That doesn't mean they don't travel, though. Some species, like the Andean flamingo, can fly hundreds of miles in one day in search of new feeding grounds.

▶ These Chilean flamingos may be looking for lower and warmer spots to gather.

Predatory Birds

▶ An African fish eagle and marabou stork fight over the carcass of a flamingo.

Python

These huge snakes kill flamingos and other prey by squeezing them to death.

Jackal

▶ These wild dogs, called jackals, like to hunt for flamingo eggs.

Baboon

▶ This large monkey takes advantage of low water levels to attack flamingos.

What's on the Menu?

Flamingos are **omnivores**—they eat both plants and animals. These birds make meals of tiny water plants, algae, and small creatures, such as pink shrimp and plankton. They also eat small bugs. Some larger species, like the American flamingo, even eat worms and fish.

In turn, flamingos are on the menu for other animals. They are easy **prey**, because they aren't strong enough to fight off predators. The safest places for flamingos are soda lakes. That's because soda lakes are too salty a **habitat** for their predators to tolerate. But flamingos are never completely safe. Many animals prey on flamingos, but their biggest threat comes from other birds.

Hunters of New World flamingos include eagles, hyenas, foxes, wildcats, hawks, and snakes. Old World flamingos may be lunch for leopards, cheetahs, jackals, baboons, and especially the marabou stork. This huge bird is twice as heavy as even the largest flamingo.

◀ A wide variety of meat-eaters prey on flamingos.

Topsy-Turvy Dining

Flamingos have a unique way of eating. First they stomp their feet in the water. That loosens food from the muddy bottom. Then they stick their heads underwater—upside down! Their flexible neck makes that easy. The birds actually eat their food underwater, too, holding their breath for a few minutes at a time. They come back out of the water for a quick breath of air, and then start all over again.

Inside each bird's bill are little membranes called lamellae, which work like combs to filter food coming in. The flamingo scoops up water, shaking its head from side to side to collect a good mix of water and food. Then it uses its tongue to push the water and mud back out through the lamellae. Bigger items are trapped inside for the bird to eat. Flamingo species that eat smaller algae and plankton have lamellae positioned very close together so the small bits of food can't escape. Larger species that eat bigger foods have lamellae that are spaced more widely.

▶ The lamellae on this bird's beak look like a comb.

lamellae

Thirsty Birds

Flamingos aren't limited to **foraging** in shallow water. Thanks to their long legs, they can also wade out to find food in deeper water. Sometimes flamingos even look for food in deep water the way ducks do. Floating on the surface of the water, they upend to reach for food—heads underwater and tails in the air.

No matter how these birds find food, they need something to wash it down! Flamingos must drink several gallons of water every single day. Freshwater is best. Sometimes flocks will travel miles and miles to find a new source of drinking water. But it's not a problem if only salt water is available. Flamingos have glands in their nostrils that help them remove the extra salt.

◀ Flamingos are at home floating on, flying over, or dunking under the water.

Moving Right Along!

Flamingos often balance on one foot. Why do they do that so often? Scientists used to think that keeping one leg out of the cool water helped flamingos stay warm. Experts also thought this position may have helped camouflage the birds among thin reeds and trees. But recent studies have revealed the truth. Standing on one leg requires less effort from the flamingo than standing on two!

Flamingos are also fabulous flyers. Other large birds, such as ostriches or penguins, are too heavy to fly. Although flamingos are big, they don't weigh much. That makes flying easy. First they gather speed by running along the ground. Then the whole flock takes off together, flying in a big V shape. They stretch out their necks and legs and flap their wide wings quickly. They can reach speeds of up to 37 miles (59 kilometers) per hour.

▶ Flamingos flap their wings quickly and continuously as they fly.

CHAPTER 3

Starting a Family

A flamingo is old enough to start its own family at about six years old. **Mating** usually happens in spring. First comes a fancy **courtship** dance. As with most other activities, the whole flock of birds dances together. The flamingos stretch out their necks and swing their heads left, then right, then left again—which is called head-flagging. They zig-zag through the water. They march. They stretch their wings, necks, and tails in a move called wing-saluting. All the birds make all of these motions together at the same time.

When two birds want to show they are interested in each other, they break away from the group and bob their heads at one another. That's their way of asking, "Will you be my mate?" Scientists believe that most flamingos have just one mate at a time.

▶ Flamingos pair off after a successful courtship dance.

Neighborhood Nesting

The flamingos in a colony build their nests close together. Both the male and female birds work together to construct a cone-shaped nest out of mud, with a shallow hollow in the middle. The mud quickly hardens in the sun. Each nest is 1 to 2 feet (.3 to .6 meters) tall, which protects it from flooding.

When the nest is finished, the female flamingo lays just one egg inside. The egg is between 3 and 3.5 inches (7.5 and 9 centimeters) long and weighs 4 to 4.9 ounces (113 to 139 grams). That's a little bigger than a large chicken egg. Even if the egg is stolen or damaged, the flamingo will not lay another until the next year.

Both parents take turns sitting on the nest. In 27 to 31 days, the egg is ready to hatch.

◀ Raising the nest off the hot ground helps keep it cool.

Chip, Cheep, Chick!

When the flamingo chick is finally ready to hatch, it can take a full day or even longer for the bird to come out of the egg. A flamingo chick uses its special egg tooth to chip its way out of the shell. While the baby bird chips, it also cheeps! The parents answer the cheeps with their own calls. This is how the birds in each flamingo family learn to recognize each other's unique sounds.

A newborn chick is about the size of a tennis ball and weighs between 2 and 3 oz. (56 and 85 g). It is covered with white or gray down, rather than feathers, and its beak is straight and red. The first food a chick is given is a high-energy milky liquid called crop milk, which the mother and father make in their throats. Later the chick will spend a few months eating **regurgitated** food from its mother and father. Feeding their chick causes the parents' pink color to fade. But when the chick begins to eat on its own, the parents get their color back again.

▶ The crop milk that parents give their chicks is bright red.

Growing Up Flamingo

About a week after it's born, the chick leaves the nest for the first time. It gathers with other young chicks in groups called crèches. The chick will continue to return to its parents at feeding time for a few months.

When the chick is about 11 weeks old, it begins getting its flight feathers. Its beak also begins to curve. But the young bird won't fly—or swim—for several more months. Until that happens, the chick is in real danger from predators. Chicks that live in soda lakes face another danger as well. Sometimes a thin band of salt builds up around the chick's ankles. The salt dries in the hot sun and hardens like cement. It's difficult for the chick to walk or fly. The young bird is likely to become prey, or to be left behind when the flock travels to a new spot. But for the chicks that make the journey, it's another step toward adulthood. These birds can live up to 40 years in the wild.

◀ Salt Lake in Turkey is home to thousands of flamingo chicks.

CHAPTER 4

Ancient Birds

Scientists know that a flamingo

ancestor named *Phoenicopterus croizeti* was one of the first birds to wade and feed in shallow water. It was not very good at flying. **Fossils** from about 40 million years ago have been found in France. Fossils from another flamingo ancestor have been found in Australia. When the Australian climate grew warmer and changed to a desert habitat, that bird completely disappeared from the continent.

Seven-million-year-old footprints of flamingo-like birds have also been found in the Andes Mountains of South America. In North America, fossils of a small-sized flamingo were found in California's Mojave Desert in the 1950s. Scientists believe that bird lived in North America until about 11,000 years ago.

All of these fossil remains are evidence that the flamingo is one of the oldest bird species on Earth.

▶ Fossils help scientists learn about present-day flamingos.

The Flamingo Family

Today, flamingos are the only living members of the Phoenicopteridae family. Scientists believe they are the distant relatives of other large wading birds, such as storks, herons, egrets, ibises, and spoonbills. Not many fossils of their common ancestors have been found, though. There is still much to discover.

Flamingos are also related to geese and to some duck species. They have the same webbed toes and waterproof feathers. But flamingos have **evolved** in a different direction. That is why scientists have given them a family name of their own.

Some people joke that the flamingos' closest modern relative is "Phoenicopterus ruber plasticus"—the plastic pink lawn flamingo! Art school graduate Don Featherstone invented this popular garden decoration in 1957.

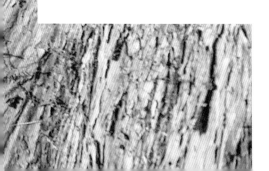

◀ Like flamingos, ibises are wading birds with large wings that live in very big colonies.

CHAPTER 5

Lore, Legends, and Lunch!

Flamingos have fascinated humans

for thousands of years. Ancient Egyptians believed these beautiful birds were the living representation of their sun god, Ra. In Rome, the most important people were given flamingo tongues to eat. There are old African legends about how flamingos came to be and why they are pink.

But what does the future look like for flamingos?

So far flamingos are doing fairly well. But there are a number of problems facing the birds. The first is **poachers**, who sell flamingos as pets, or sell their eggs or meat for people to eat. In some areas, tourists can also be a problem. They can get too close in order to take photos. When flamingos are bothered, they may leave their nests and eggs behind. This puts the next generation at risk.

▶ This painting of a Turkish man with his pet is hundreds of years old.

Don't Harm Our Habitat

The biggest threat facing flamingos is the danger to their habitat. Pollution from **sewage** and increasing land development means fewer safe breeding places for the flamingos. Every year, fewer flamingos are born. For a time, people even believed that James's flamingos were **extinct**. Then a group of them was found in South America in the 1950s. Today, the smallest and most at-risk population of flamingos is the Andean species.

Mining is another big problem. Sodium carbonate, which is used to make glass, toothpaste, detergent, and other products, is being mined from soda lakes. To get the sodium carbonate, water is pumped into the lake. When the water **evaporates**, the salt left behind is cut into blocks and then removed. That makes the lakes evaporate faster, and it leaves flamingos with less water for feeding and fewer salt islands to gather on. Scientists worry that mining may cause flamingos to become **endangered**.

◀ A worker harvests large amounts of salt from a soda lake.

Helping Flamingos Flourish

People are working hard to protect flamingos, and they are making a real difference. In North America, hunting and habitat destruction had reduced the population to only about 20,000 flamingos. Then **conservation** efforts began. Now there are more than 800,000 of these birds living in Florida alone.

In South America, Bolivia and Chile both have national flamingo reserves. Some nesting grounds around the world are also protected now, with park rangers on patrol to keep them safe. Meanwhile, scientists are studying flamingo species all over the world and developing action plans. If we pay attention, these marvelous, colorful birds will continue to bring joy and beauty to our world for many years to come.

▶ Flamingos do well in zoos, and, in fact, live longer there than they would in the wild.

Flamingo Family Tree

Flamingos are birds. They are warm-blooded animals that have feathers and can fly. They lay eggs, from which their babies are born. Scientists believe that more than 150 million years ago, birds evolved from small dinosaurs that eventually developed wings and became small enough to fly. This diagram shows how flamingos are related to other seabirds. The closer together two animals are on the tree, the more similar they are.

Geese
waterfowl that are larger than ducks and have longer necks

Grebes
freshwater diving birds that rarely or never fly

Ducks
birds with webbed feet that live in salt- and freshwater

Auks
small seabirds with short legs and webbed feet

Ancestor of all Seabirds

Note: Animal photos are not to scale.

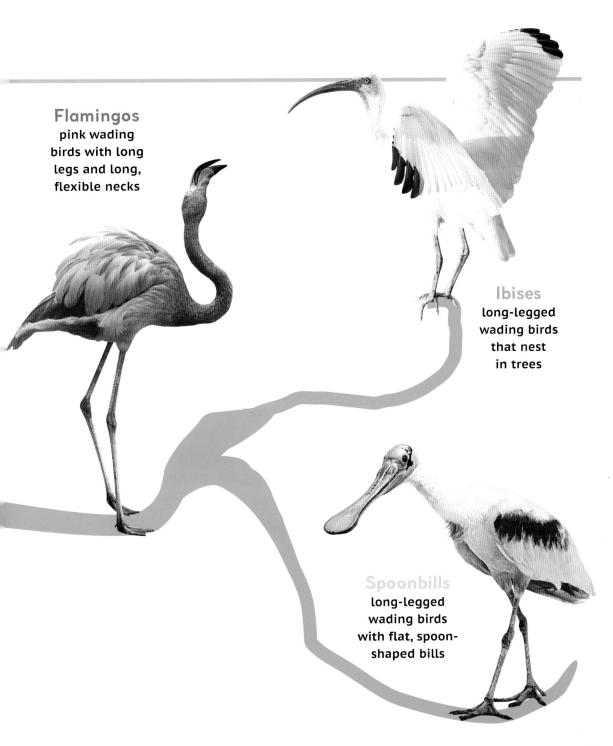

Flamingos
pink wading
birds with long
legs and long,
flexible necks

Ibises
long-legged
wading birds
that nest
in trees

Spoonbills
long-legged
wading birds
with flat, spoon-
shaped bills

43

Words to Know

A .... **ancestor** *(ANN-ses-tur)* family member who lived long ago

C .... **camouflage** *(KAM-uh-flahzh)* the disguising or hiding of something by making it blend into its background

conservation *(kahn-sur-VAY-shun)* the protection of valuable things, especially forests, wildlife, or natural resources

courtship *(KORT-ship)* the act of seeking a mate

E .... **endangered** *(en-DAYN-juhrd)* a plant or animal in danger of becoming extinct, usually because of human activity

estuaries *(ES-choo-er-eez)* the wide parts of rivers, where they join the ocean

evaporates *(ee-VAP-or-ayts)* changes into vapor from a liquid state

evolved *(i-VAHLVD)* changed slowly and naturally over time

extinct *(ik-STINGKT)* no longer found alive

F .... **foraging** *(FOR-ij-ing)* searching for food by hunting, fishing, or gathering

fossils *(FAH-suhls)* bones, shells, or other traces of an animal or plant from millions of years ago, preserved as rock

G .... **gland** *(GLAND)* an organ in the body that produces a substance to be used or given off (such as sweat)

H .... **habitat** *(HAB-i-tat)* the place where an animal or plant is usually found

L ········· lagoons *(luh-GOONZ)* small freshwater lakes near larger lakes or rivers

M ········· mating *(MAY-ting)* the act of pairing a male and female in order to reproduce

migrate *(MYE-grate)* to move to another area or climate at a particular time of year

O ········· omnivores *(AHM-ni-vorz)* animals or people that eat both plants and meat for food

P ········· poachers *(POHCH-uhrz)* people who hunt or fish illegally on someone else's property

predators *(PRED-uh-tuhrz)* animals that hunt other animals for food

preening *(PREEN-ing)* grooming and cleaning feathers with a beak

prey *(PRAY)* an animal that is hunted by another animal for food

R ········· regurgitated *(ree-GERJ-uh-tay-ted)* swallowed or partially digested food that is brought up to the mouth again

S ········· sewage *(SOO-ij)* liquid and solid waste that is carried into bodies of water by sewers and drains

species *(SPEE-sheez)* one of the groups into which animals and plants are divided; members of the same species can mate and have offspring

W ········· wetlands *(WET-landz)* land where there is a lot of moisture in the soil; these include swamps, bayous, and marshes

Find Out More

BOOKS

- Gish, Melissa. *Flamingos* (Living Wild). Mankato, MN: Creative Education, 2015.
- Malone, Jean M. *Flamingos* (All Aboard Science Reader). New York: Grosse & Dunlap, 2009.

WEB PAGES

- http://animals.sandiegozoo.org/animals/flamingo

  Information about all aspects of flamingos, presented by the San Diego Zoo.
- www.bioexpedition.com/american-flamingo/

  This site offers basic facts about flamingos along with photos.
- https://birdeden.com/interesting-facts-about-flamingos

  Visit this site for quick flamingo facts and photos.

FILM

- *The Crimson Wing: Mystery of the Flamingos*. Walt Disney Studios, 2008.

  This British-American nature documentary features fantastic footage of lesser flamingos in Tanzania.

Facts for Now

Visit this Scholastic Web site for more information on flamingos:
www.factsfornow.scholastic.com Enter the keyword **Flamingos**

Index

Index *(continued)*

About the Author

Jodie Shepherd is the author of dozens of both fiction and nonfiction children's books and is an editor at Sesame Workshop. She is an avid, though totally amateur, birdwatcher.